M.J. GALLANT

Thoughts From Reconstruction

Finding light in the dark, signal in the noise, and reconstruction in the deconstruction.

Donna and Alan Gallant
My Mom and Dad
Who Raised Me
And Gifted Me Life

Ah, but a man's reach should exceed
his grasp, or what's a heaven for?

Robert Browning, Andrea del Sarto

Contents

Acknowledgement

*Gravity keeps my head down, or is it maybe shame
at being so young and being so vain?*
-Manic Street Preachers, If You Tolerate This

Thank you to God, who is who He is, for the sacrifice of His Son, Jesus the Christ, for the forgiveness of my sins, and for His Holy Spirit, seal until the Great Day, and for life and breath and opportunity to act in service to the King in the building of the Kingdom.

Thank you to the many who have influenced my life. First, my mother and father for raising me as well and better than any child could hope or wish.

Thank you to my sister and my brother. My sister for showing interest in my writings and laughing hysterically at my silly stories. My brother for acting like a true brother and inviting me along as a duo.

Thank you to my friends who indulge my appetite for deep, meaningful conversation. Whether over frivolous video games, relaxing in a hot tub under starry skies, or hiking nature trails. These conversations, and the way in which ideas find their energy there, carry great weight and value for me.

Thank you to former pastors, our own and visiting, who have put great passion and deeply insightful thought and care into their sermons without knowing just how the Holy Spirit was going to use it.

Thank you to the fallen faith leaders who I looked up to as examples. While you stood, I consider that you spoke largely Good News and Bible truth and that makes all the difference. We all fall and mercy triumphs.

Thank you to the thinkers and the conversationalists like Jordan B. Peterson, Paul VanderKlay, Jonathan Pageau, Douglas Murray, Tom Holland (the historian not Spider-Man) and others in that group who put great thought into the deeper issues of faith and meaning in our times. They show, by example, how to have conversations that aren't just debates to be won or lost but that provide real, meaningful value.

Thank you to all of the Creation ministries, such as Creation Ministries International, especially, for the delightfully fun, informing, and faith-building Creation Magazine, Answers in Genesis, and Institute for Creation Research. Thank you to their speakers, as well, who put the personal and human face on each organization. It has been solid, robust, biblical creation material that has perhaps most reliably given me the logical framework and the confidence to research into and trust in biblical authority wherever it is challenged by the issues of the day.

Thank you to Cassandra Thomas for the gift of the painting

which is now the artwork on the cover of this book. I had nearly lost hope of finding a visual rich enough to match what was in my head when I happened to look again at the painting and knew that, of course, this was all along the piece that would illustrate this book.

And thank you, reader, for your valuable time, energy, and attention spent reading this book. It means a lot to me that people find value in what I write. I hope that the Holy Spirit uses these frail words in a way that honors God in your life and mine.

Soli Deo Gloria

1

Inspiration

*The thing that scares most off the hero's journey
is that it has a long stretch that looks like the zero's
journey.*

In my estimation, I was raised very well. I would never have guessed any of my family, let alone myself, might experience deconstruction.

Conservative and regular church attendance were contrasted and complemented by a scientist father and teacher mother, both who encouraged critical thinking and open-mindedness. My father was never afraid to vocalize controversial takes, particularly ones regarding the faith. My mother ensured we had reliable Christian material with which to stand our faith upon. Our family, including my sister and brother, have gone on to lead faithful, Christian families and lives.

And yet here we are. Perhaps you are, too.

This is a book about rebuilding out of the ruins of a post-postmodern world. The journey of reconstruction takes on truth, faith, meaning, and learning how to know right from wrong.

As I realized mine was, your view of Christianity might be heavily influenced by the Ten Commandments and the Law from the Old Testament (Old Covenant). You know: Do this, don't do that, acceptable, unacceptable, right, wrong...

I invite you to come along as I revisit my journey. You'll come across the twists and turns, the side-streets and alleys, and the hills and valleys I ventured through in seeking the answers to some of the biggest questions we all carry.

I have ruminated and written over many years, hashing out questions, trying to get to something firm, something I can stand on, something real.

Our journey will take the form of a canvas painted with words, thoughts, essays, with dab and stroke, so that, when we have made the last touch, we'll be able to step back and look upon wild dabs and strokes, erratic, irrational, even, but ultimately coalescing into a rich, lush, landscape of soul-satisfying meaning[1].

We're going to stroll down a road marked on either side with the billboards and milestones of my written explorations. The first step of a thousand miles must be to orient ourselves. So, we'll set the stage to give you a frame of reference so you can better understand what's to come.

Once we have that covered, we'll go down the rabbit hole of rationality, irrationality, and the paradoxes of our beliefs. We'll resurface and see how upside-down the world of faith really can be by taking a look at the Kingdom of Heaven, who Jesus *really* said were blessed, and our predictably pathetic attempts at trying to 'be perfect as your Heavenly Father is perfect'.

When you're ready, we'll deep dive what Jesus was really saying when he said, *"This cup is the new covenant in my blood, which is poured out for you."* (Luke 22:20b)

But to start, we'll begin near the end, taking a look at what the humble prism can teach us about truth and how we can go about finding it.

This is a book about revisiting, reorienting, recalibrating, and regenerating.

We're going to explore reconstruction out of deconstruction[2].

2

Prisms and Principles

I believe in Christianity as I believe that the sun has risen: not only because I see it, but because by it I see everything else. –C.S. Lewis

Prisms reveal a rainbow of colored light when placed in the path of white light. The prism lens shows us the multi-colored light that was there all along. Looking at the bands of colors can tell us something about the original light and tracing the colors back through the prism can tell us something about the source. Prisms, then, can be seen as a lens for interpreting light and source.

As with the prism light, we can study the things in our world across many bands of color, many areas of study, and they each contribute some understanding to the whole understanding. And, as with focusing only on one band of color to the exclusion of others, we make the same mistake when we try to build the whole understanding from only some understanding.

When I look at any given collection of what seem to be related things, my intuition is always asking, *"How do these all fit together?"* Many things don't need to fit together, of course, but then there are some that demand out of their very being that they *must* fit together. Sometimes it matters little if you can fit everything together while sometimes it means the world. One of these times arises in trying to understand the sum of the writings, claims, and ramifications that is the Holy Bible.

Astronomy and Approach

Astronomers have long studied the stars using light from which they can deduce many things about the stars, themselves, such as chemical composition, temperature, density, mass, distance, and luminosity. Astronomers can use even non-visible light, such as ultraviolet, x-ray, infrared, and radio frequencies to discover even more.

Each band of color is an area of study with specific analysis and results, work and rewards. Visible light analysis can reveal types of matter such as solids and gasses, and hotter and cooler temperatures. X-rays are used to reveal comets via solar winds. Radio and infrared can help reveal complex molecules in space.

> *The heavens declare the glory of God; the skies proclaim the work of his hands. Day after day they pour forth speech; night after night they reveal knowledge. They have no speech, they use no words; no sound is heard from them. Yet their voice goes out into all the earth, their words to the ends of the world. -Psalms 19:1-4*

The stars have no speech yet they have voice, use no words yet words go out, no sound is heard yet *day after day they pour forth speech.*

Selah.

Tack and Tangent

Jesus gave us simple truths and commands and by the combination explosion of mere men attempting to comprehend them we have come through many roads of knowledge.

> Love God and Neighbor. Preach the Gospel and Make Disciples. Mercy Triumphs over Judgment. -Matthew 22:37-40, Matthew 28:18-20, James 2:12-13

We have come through Greek exceptionalism, Roman pragmatism, Medieval Scholasticism, Enlightenment Rationalism, Modernist Empiricism, Postmodern Deconstruction, and, our present mood, a sort of unholy spiritual-nihilist hybrid.

Each period gave its input on how to understand what we see around us and each new period sometimes took the gold and left the dross and sometimes forgot to know what was gold and what was dross.

From the many great minds of every time we have expanded the breadth of techniques with which the angles of a phenomena may be approached. We now look at any given body of knowledge from many different sides and cross-sections. From surface-level to symbolic, psychological to sociological, grammar to presentation, speaker to audience, intent to reception, prose to poetry, history to apocalypse.

Every angle of approach is an area of study with specific analysis and results, work and rewards. The surface can reveal immediate takeaways. The psychological can reveal inner, personal truths. The sociological can reveal outer, communal behaviors. Grammar can reveal literary goals and presentation invites innate response. Speaker and audience can reveal personal and group position and communication dynamics. Intent and reception can reveal how communication is crafted to deliver meaning. Prose and poetry can reveal complexity of thought and emotion. And history and apocalypse can reveal the past, how the past was understood, and how the future is foreseen.

One or more, or all, of these levels can exist and be true at the same time. But how do they relate to each other when they co-exist? Must they agree or can they contradict each other? And how can we even know they are actually present?

Relations and Rapports

> *The way back from postmodernism is to realize we can trace back the deconstruction to the construction as we can trace back prism light from dissociation to association*[3].

What is the true understanding of a thing if more than one understanding can apply? The Prism Principle applies. Experience and investigation teaches us that multiple levels of meaning, angles of approach, do not and can not exist *independent* of each other. They must all come back to their source.

Astronomy vividly teaches us that there are many dimensions to a star's light and each dimension teaches us something unique. Visible light can tell the speed of a spinning object and infrared can tell us about complex molecules in its space or in the atmosphere of planets the light travels through.

But if your visible light is telling you a planet is spinning faster than the ability for complex molecules to stay in its atmosphere, without being ripped away, then you must question whether you understand the meaning of each band of color: You will try to resolve and harmonize your findings within the bounds of reason and reality.

You might even question how you know the differing aspects of analysis are there to begin with. In astronomical spectroscopy you would ensure you have identified the tell-tale signs of each area. That is, you would ensure the light spectrum is or is not present, its intensity, and many other properties.

So, too, with any area of interest, including a text like the Bible.

Take, for instance, the type of text, whether prose, poetry, wisdom, history, or apocalypse. Prose may begin by narration and exhibit plot or character arcs. Poetry often includes repetition of words, structures, or ideas, rhythm, rhyme, and visual elements when written. Wisdom may include abstract and intangible behoovements and axioms of oughts and ought nots and bewares. History will include dates, times, durations, periods, people, places, and events. And apocalypse text will look to a future time, often using coded language and symbols, and often with a message of hope or warning or both.

The text will tell you what it is intended to represent, whether one thing or many, just like light will tell you what it represents by its amplitude, period, phase shift, and frequency.

Light and Luminescence

God...who alone is immortal and who lives in unapproach-able light, whom no one has seen or can see. -1 Timothy 6:15b-16a

Let's take, God, for example, who, convenient to our prism example, is described as *living in inapproachable light, whom no one has seen* and yet is given any number of characteristics and descriptions.

God is described as and revealed in act to be infinite, self-existing, and without origin; immutable, never-changing; self-sufficient and needing nothing; omnipotent, all-powerful; omniscient, all-knowing; omnipresent, always everywhere; perfectly wise; faithful and unchanging; good and kind; just, right, and righteous; merciful and compassionate; gracious; loving; Holy, separate, and perfect; beautiful, great, and glori-ous.

We can now understand how it is that one who *lives in inapproach-able light* can be revealed to be a kaleidoscope of characteristics: God's being emanates like light through the prism of Creation which exhibits his attributes like shifted bands of color through the elements of the material and immaterial world.

And every band of God's being is an area of study with specific analysis and results, work and rewards.

Study the stars and glimpse of God's order and majesty. Study God's creatures and see a hint of His creativity and caring. Study His earth, sky, and plants, and perceive part of God's intelligence and glory.

Now follow those banded colors of God's being, step back and trace those colors as they converge and become unified, and see how they speak to and lead you to something greater, yet simpler.

You are looking back through the prism of Creation to the Source who *lives in inapproachable light.*

Hues and Horizons

> *For in him all things were created: things in heaven and on earth, visible and invisible, whether thrones or powers or rulers or authorities; all things have been created through him and for him. -Colossians 1:16*

Sometimes it matters little if you can fit everything together while sometimes it means the world.

Let us study, then, all of the world, God's Written Word, and God, Himself, through all the areas that can be studied, all those bands of color: The surface-level, the symbolic, the psychological, the sociological, the grammar, the presentation, the speaker, the audience, the intent, the reception, the prose, the poetry, the history, the revelation.

Follow those bands of color and be lead to where they coalesce, overlap, combine, and become one.

Look to the prism of Creation and see the colors converge, the many become one, impure become pure, and diversity become unity.

We will then find a more complete picture, a fuller understanding, and something greater, yet simpler.

> *I believe in Christianity as I believe that the sun has risen: not only because I see it, but because by it I see everything else. –C.S. Lewis*

Selah.

3

Do you believe in God? Provide your reasoning.

A very good question to ask was asked on Twitter:

Do you believe in God/a higher power? Please provide reasoning below. -@LayahHeilpern, Twitter[4]

I thought that was a really good question and I thought it might be helpful to sum up my answer in a reply[5]:

Good question. All experience tells us there must be a "God". Or else nothing should exist at all. What that God is is up to you to find out. The Christian God provides the most complete, coherent, meaningful, and believable God across all levels of analysis.

All experience tells us there must be a "God"

What do I mean, *all experience tells us there must be a "God"*? All material and immaterial phenomena speak of a source, a starting point. Things like the design of the universe, the fine-tuned nature of reality, theories of origins, cause and effect, information theory: All of these speak to a "God". The next logical question is *what is that God?*

Or else nothing should exist at all

Without a God, there's no reason for anything to exist at all.

We haven't defined *God* yet. Such a "God" might be nature, itself, but then where did Nature come from and what properties of Nature give it the ability to produce the intelligence and complexity we find all around us?

It seems that without a God, whatever that may be at this point, nothing should exist at all. And I don't mean that in the double-speak way of modern science where they speak of 'quantum fluctuations' as "nothing": Those are "something". I mean actually void, nil, nothing, "no thing".

Whatever ultimately caused all this *something* is God.

What that God is is up to you to find out

This might sound flippant but if a God is a logical conclusion to draw from existence then it's probably the most important question you could ever ask and answer.

You should investigate God. Is God the universe? Is God all of us? Is God Zeus? Is God Allah? Is God the Judeo-Christian God?

The Christian God provides the most complete, coherent, meaningful, and believable God across all levels of analysis

My answer is that the God revealed in the Judeo-Christian faith answers more questions, and by far, than any other.

The Christian God's story begins at the beginning, reveals Himself constantly and consistently throughout all of our history, and ends at the end, which is, itself, a new beginning.

The Christian God is coherent, understandable, relatable, followable, and makes sense of the world around us. He reveals Himself to us and in a way that we can understand Him and also communicate with him.

The Christian God is meaningful and brings both gravity and levity to life by providing the context, source, ambition for life, and the relationship which defines all other relationships.

The Christian God is believable and brings sense and reason to bear on our world, the nature of reality, our history, more so than any other theory of origins.

From surface-level to symbolic, psychological to sociological–and in Christian scriptures–grammar to presentation, speaker to audience, intent to reception, prose to poetry, history to apocalypse: The Christian God and His revelation to us provides the most complete, coherent, meaningful, and believable

God across all levels of analysis.

For God so loved the world that he gave his one and only Son, that whoever believes in him shall not perish but have eternal life. –John 3:16

4

We have to go back

This time around things came a little bit easier. What a trip. What story telling. I more often had "aha!" moments and more than a few head-nods to the writer's foreshadowing.

I'm talking about Lost, the ABC television show that enthralled (and eventually enraged) audiences from 2004 to 2010.

For having gone as long as it did, for having kept almost all of its cast members the entire time, for having a grand story arch they stuck to and finished, and for the sheer magnitude of the undertaking, I can't think of a better television series.

So, if "*we have to go back*", here are my main take-aways from the show's six-year run...

Father Figures

Wow. Where do you start with this one? Did any character in that show have a healthy father figure? Not really? Why is that? Having been blessed to grow up in a healthy family with a loving mom and dad, and having known families without that and what tends to happen, this was a glaring point of commentary in the show. Trust me. You don't keep hitting the same plot device over the head without intending to say something about it.

From Jack's alcoholic father, Kate's abusive father, Claire's son's run-away father, Hurley's absentee father, Shannon's missing father, John's no-show father, Ben's neglectful father, to Jacob and his brother's unknown father, the show is rife, again and again, with father figure issues. Episodes were even named referencing "daddy issues".

Why so much emphasis on father figures, bad ones, at that?

I tend to think it was a statement against God. There is a train of thought that considers God to be an absentee father. If that's true, you'd expect them to come down on one side of the question or the other and how that played out in the lives of the characters. What seems to have played out, given the idea that the sideways universe was a sort purgatory[6] which wasn't really real, is that it would seem most of the fathers never did become good fathers, except maybe for Michael but did he turn out well in reality? He was stuck on the island after committing suicide in the real-world due to guilt about telling his son what he did on the island to get them off. So, bad father figures beget bad father figures, I guess?

Man of Science vs Man of Faith

An interesting development, one I wouldn't expect from our naturalistic, materialistic culture was which side of the old romantic versus naturalist philosophy triumphed in the end.

John and Jack were pitted against each other early on as a "man of faith" and a "man of science". For seasons Jack rejected John's claims of fate and destiny but by the end he was a complete convert. I didn't expect this. Given that our culture is so into 'science', to the level of faith, I figured the writers would somehow make that philosophy come out on top. Amazingly, they didn't. If Lost was a battle between romanticism and naturalism, faith and science, then, surprisingly, romanticism won.

One book I'll recommend any day of the week is Saving Leonardo[7] by Nancy Pearcey. It's an unabashedly Christian look at the driving philosophies since the Enlightenment[8] in the arts, the sciences, literature, music, film, etc. One thing it does very well is describe how our modern philosophies are simply renditions of the same old "there's more than we can see" versus "this is all we can see".

Why did faith win out in the end? Why did they write it like that? Maybe because, although our modern, western culture loves cold, hard science, it *is* very cold and hard and we like to think that we have a soft, warm, 'good' side to us, too. Love wins in the end, right? Or maybe the cold conclusions of materialism just don't make for good television? I don't know but it does make for a better story – and that should make you think a little.

Existential Angst

You'll notice that the church at the end, where all the survivors gather to "move on", is a multi-faith church. It has symbols from all different faiths. These are actually real types of places. What you have, then, is a statement, perhaps subtle to some but painfully obvious to others, that all beliefs lead to...well, something good. The show didn't really elaborate, but those who were not ready were kept in their painful circumstances. The problem with "all ways get to the same place" is that they don't. Some ways lead to the mountains, some ways lead to the sea. Some ways claim one thing, some ways claim the opposite. The law of non-contradiction[9] arises and so one of them has to be wrong. They can all be wrong, but they can't all be right.

The writers were clearly steeped in and serving a post-modern, western audience, and that's where you're going to run into trouble if you want to say anything really meaningful. In the end, Lost was itself lost in its own metaphysics, just as the culture it was reflecting is lost in our mixed up, tumbled, confused ideas about right and wrong, how to find meaning, what makes a person good, and all the other big questions.

The End

So, after six years, 121 episodes, an epic, time-traveling, universe-fraying survivor story, what do we take away? Why was it so powerful if it was so meaningless? Where do we go from here?

We have to go back.

We have to go back to where we lost the way, to where we crashed on this island of contradictions and meaninglessness. We have to go back to a time before we grew up not even knowing we were being conditioned to live in this personal purgatory where we've forgotten there is such a thing as redemption. We have to go back to when we still believed in fate and destiny. We have to go back to the beginning. We have to go back to our constant.

> *Jesus answered, "I am the way and the truth and the life. No one comes to the Father except through me." –John 14:6*

> *Jesus answered, "You say that I am a king. In fact, the reason I was born and came into the world is to testify to the truth. Everyone on the side of truth listens to me." –John 18:37*

> *For God so loved the world that he gave his one and only Son, that whoever believes in him shall not perish but have eternal life. –John 3:16*

We have to go back to God.

5

Preparation

I don't feel obliged to believe that the same God who has endowed us with sense, reason, and intellect has intended us to forgo their use. –Galileo Galilei

Somewhere around my early twenties I realized that if I was going to believe the faith I had been brought up in then my faith would have to stand up to being challenged[10].

So, I tasked myself with investigating the flaws, contradictions, and errors that are always brought up around Christianity and the Bible. Like how the Bible and its Books was supposedly 'selected' by a small group of Roman Catholics with an agenda. Or, parts of the Bible that are contradicted by other parts of the Bible. Or, outright mistakes in the Bible, perhaps about geography, mathematics, historical figures, or its account of Creation at odds with Evolution.

This was the early days of the Internet, before social media, when people frequented discussion forums, made personal websites, and wrote personal blogs. I started responding to Atheist questions on discussion forums and started a personal website where I wrote things now lost even to the Internet's memory.

As questions came up, I pushed myself to research the answers and quickly discovered a number of resources that largely dealt with all of these issues before. Places like GotQuestions.org, Creation.com, and good old fashion search engines turned up people who had already tackled these issues and provided the logic for how to respond and uphold the reliability and robustness of the Bible.

As it turns out, and to paraphrase a famous saying, there are no new questions, only old questions posed to new people. I would discover that nearly every issue brought up had been dealt with already by others, sometimes for centuries, sometimes for millennia.

I wasn't always as confident in finding the Bible-supporting answers as I am now. There was a time when each new question struck a note of panicked doubt. Maybe my faith really was imaginary, the Bible really was just written by mere men, and God didn't really exist. It took years to build up the confidence out of experience that any new question that came my way would already have a satisfactory answer.

So, I hope you can now now understand a little of where I'm coming from. My story isn't unusual. Most go through the same thing. Many are scared and don't engage the questions. Most won't experience the delight of finding answers that support their faith.

Even fewer come to understand the deeper and richer nature of the faith that lies beyond those questions. Over time, I gained a sense of peace from all of this investigation that revealed highly reasonable, highly satisfying responses to critiques of the faith.

But some ideas refuse to give us peace until we find peace in the reasonableness of the unreasonable.

6

The Unreasonable Doubt of Rational Deduction

Science employs the five natural senses, sight, sound, smell, taste, and touch, or technological extensions or assistances of these, in order to understand the existence in which we reside. Because science relies only on what we know to reliably and repeatedly reveal the truth, we call this objective inquiry or rational thought. But this is only rational if you're blissfully unaware of all senses to the contrary. Science, as the ultimate source of truth, is the abandonment of reason because it ignores rationality, itself.

By objectifying the senses, taking them out of the subjective, the man, we lose the qualities of the mind, which not only processes the data from the five senses, but also applies another sense to the compilation of all those data streams. The mind applies rational deduction. That is, the mind reasons.

Reasoning is not simply an analysis of the five senses. It is a sense, in its own right, as it draws upon a confluence of knowledge, experience, intuition, and the other common senses, and tells us things contrary to what those common senses would have us believe.

We find, then, that we have an additional sense which can not be separated from the man. In separating the senses which can be separated from the man, and ignoring what can not, science, well-meaning and profitable though it be, has seen fit to draw conclusions missing the most important sense of them all. Science has not seen it unreasonable to abandon reason.

The only thing that gives a man reason is his mind. Science has taken reason out of the picture and has thus lost its mind.

So, it is not an over-simplified and reductive perception of reality that allows us to understand our world but a complex arsenal of rational tools. Science has over-simplified its toolset and become irrational.

Well stated by Einstein, "everything should be made as simple as possible, but no simpler."

7

The Paradox In Which All Men Believe

There is a paradox to the Christian faith which concerns the very origins of our existence. The paradox consists of realizing that everything has a cause, hence our existence was created by God. But everything has a cause; Then God must have had a cause; So, really, that *cause* is God; And that intermediate "God" wasn't really God.

We don't talk like that. We say that God created our existence and that God simply is. He had no beginning and has no cause. He is self-existent.

Science, however, theorizes any number of ideas in which a natural existence can be the cause of itself. Hence, the infinite collapse and explosion of our universe in the big bang, or the multiverse theories. Can either of these be considered to have *been* already? Or are "existence" and "universe" considered one and so the existence simply *is?* You can abstract, extrapolate, interpolate and push back what *is* further and further out but you must satisfy the law that all *this* was *caused.* And that is the paradox. All things have a cause except the origins of what *is*.

One can start to see that this irrationality is actually the rationality claimed by modernity.

I use, in this instance, Christianity as the symbol for all religions, for the defining principle of all religion is faith, and Science as the symbol for rationality. It doesn't matter that Christianity is different than Buddhism , but that modern thought differentiates itself from religion because it perceives irrationality. It doesn't matter that Science is not the only system of rational thought, but that we generally differentiate what is science and what is religion by considering one rational and one not. They represent the two halves of the great chasm separating man's mind from himself.

Once you've gotten past the issue of knowing the paradox of origins, you must rationally come to the conclusion that, because there is no reason for existence to be, *at all*, there must be a cause of our existence. This cause, no matter how far back or how many iterations out you push this, must be final. This final cause has chosen to reveal itself not through natural test (our five senses; that is, scientific inquiry), but rather through rational deduction. That is, you must *rationally* deduce that the origins of existence are *irrationally* discovered. You must believe in a paradox to be reasonable. You must become irrational to become rational.

That this God would choose to be revealed this way should give us pause for thought.

8

Illustration

*It is always simple to fall; there are an infinity of angles
at which one falls, only one at which one stands. - G.K. Chesterton*

My early days as a Christian were filled with upright examples—but one by one they came tumbling down. This, as you might well guess, contributes to a certain dissonance of faith. Some find it easy to pass those thoughts by and live life contented. I am not one of those.

Even though many pillars of my faith have fallen, I was able to see the truth in what they were saying. I was able to take the gold and leave the dross, you might put it. I realized that what drew me to these people was the truthfulness and value of what they were speaking: In spite of falling in the Flesh, they spoke the Spirit truth. In this way, I had something real to cling to when my heroes fell.

I have been blessed to sit under the teaching of thinkers who showed truly inspired takes on scriptures I had long glossed over. It was these novel readings that shifted my viewpoint just enough that I was able to gain something more. And that something more would be stepping stones to understanding my faith at a deeper and more satisfying level.

In one particularly memorable Sunday service, I listened as our pastor taught the Beatitudes, from Matthew 5. He was able to show us that, rather than some kind of list of proverbs, or atomized nuggets of wisdom, the Beatitudes form a whole and each verse builds on the one before. That's when, per my odd sensibilities, I decided to read it backwards.

Also in Matthew 5, we find Jesus' words, "Be perfect, therefore, as your heavenly Father is perfect." It sounds so nice. So right. So...wait, what? Be *perfect* as God is perfect? I had always left that verse alone with a haunting feeling of falling short. Then, one day, things started to click and I had to write and figure out what was meant by another scripture: *Christ in you, the hope of glory.*

In another Sunday sermon, our pastor talked about the Kingdom of Heaven: What it is, where it is, and when it is. Just setting it in those contexts piqued my interest. He phrased one thought this way: The Kingdom of Heaven is wherever the King reigns, and wherever the King reigns is where His Will is done. We all have this sense of anxious expectation for the return of Christ to usher in the Kingdom of Heaven, and that's part of the picture, but Jesus' own words reveal to us something even more mind expanding.

These three easy-to-miss ideas began to form a change of mind in me, the beginnings of a paradigm shift, and they solidified ideas that would help me to understand what's really going on with our faith, what constitutes our faith, and what the New Covenant was really all about.

9

Those who mourn are blessed: Reading scripture backwards.

A few weeks ago our pastor taught on the Beatitudes, Matthew 5:3-12, and he highlighted something I hadn't really considered before. The verses from 3 to 12 are not simply separate sayings, like little nuggets of wisdom. They're not like some parts you might find in Proverbs, superficially a list of wise but standalone sayings. Instead, they form a whole and each verse builds on the one before.

Have a quick read through with that in mind and we'll pick up after,

> *Jesus began to teach them,*
>
> *"Blessed are the poor in spirit,*
> *for theirs is the kingdom of heaven.*
> *Blessed are those who mourn,*
> *for they will be comforted.*
> *Blessed are the meek,*

for they will inherit the earth.
Blessed are those who hunger and thirst for righteous-
ness,
for they will be filled.
Blessed are the merciful,
for they will be shown mercy.
Blessed are the pure in heart,
for they will see God.
Blessed are the peacemakers,
for they will be called children of God.
Blessed are those who are persecuted because of righ-
teousness,
for theirs is the kingdom of heaven.

"Blessed are you when people insult you, persecute you
and falsely say all kinds of evil against you because of
me. Rejoice and be glad, because great is your reward in
heaven, for in the same way they persecuted the prophets
who were before you.

–Matthew 5:3–12

The first thing that struck me was that these people were
"blessed." *Blessed?!*

Maybe they were blessed because each 'bad thing' was followed
up by a comforting thing, like "Blessed are those who mourn,
for they will be comforted," but that's a little morbid, isn't?

If we put up with mourning we'll be blessed by being comforted?
But I couldn't get around the wording, "Blessed are those who

mourn..." *Blessed are those.* You are, I am, *blessed* when we mourn.

> blessed
> adjective
> 1. consecrated; sacred; holy; sanctified: the Blessed Sacrament.
> 2. worthy of adoration, reverence, or worship: the Blessed Trinity.
> 3. divinely or supremely favored; fortunate: to be blessed with a strong, healthy body; blessed with an ability to find friends.
> 4. blissfully happy or contented.
> *-Dictionary.com entry for "blessed"*

Read as a whole, I started to wonder, *who lives all these things?* And, of course, whenever you ask something like that, especially about virtues, the answer is usually *Jesus*! So, I began to see the life of Christ in those words.

Christ was poor in spirit, downtrodden, misspoken to, looked down upon. Christ mourned – for Lazarus, for Jerusalem, and certainly for the many he healed of sickness and sin, for his family because He knew where He was headed, for humanity as He hung on the cross because He knew who would ignore His Offer. Christ was meek – He didn't respond in power when tempted by Satan in the wilderness. Christ hungered and thirsted for righteousness – He stayed behind at the temple as a child because 'He had to be about His Father's business.' Christ was merciful – He had mercy on those he healed of sickness and sin. Christ was pure in heart – He lived a perfect life, to die a perfect sacrifice. Christ was a peacemaker – He didn't incite violence from His followers, He went to death peacefully. He was persecuted for righteousness' sake – He went to the cross because He taught true righteousness.

Christ is our example. He wasn't teaching His followers something He wasn't already going through.

What really struck me though was, as I was trying to understand if each verse was really a step in a series, I wanted to confirm that by seeing if it could be read backwards. That's when I started to see it like this,

- ***Blessed are those who mourn, for they are poor in spirit.*** It was true. Those who understand their true, sinful condition before a Holy, sinless God, recognize they are *poor in spirit* and they *mourn* because of it.
- ***Blessed are the meek, for they mourn.*** A true mourner, understanding his real, sin condition, is always *meek* – who, being honest of his condition, would not ask, *"Who can save me now?"*
- ***Blessed are those who hunger and thirst after righteousness, for they are meek.*** The meek will admit they can't do it on their own, they are not prideful, and they will search for what will cure them.
- ***Blessed are the merciful, for they hunger and thirst after righteousness.*** Those who find righteousness understand the mercy given to them in the sacrifice of Jesus Christ on the cross, for their sins – and they show mercy out of grateful hearts and true understanding of the gift they have received.
- ***Blessed are the pure in heart, for they are merciful.*** The Book

of James says, "*Mercy triumphs over judgment.*" You will only find the pure in heart when you find the one who is also merciful for 'they have the Spirit of Christ living in them, Christ, the One who is Mercy' (Romans 8:9-11).

- ***Blessed are the peacemakers, for they are pure in heart.*** Those who are pure in heart will also make peace with their neighbor because they are merciful, they know that strife would only harm their brother or sister.

- ***Blessed are those who are persecuted because of righteousness, for they are peacemakers.*** The peacemakers will be persecuted for their righteousness exactly because their persecutors are not *peacemakers*, because they are not *pure in heart*, because they are not *merciful*, because they are not *hungry and thirsty for righteousness*, because they are not *meek*, because they are not *mourning*, because they do not recognize their *poverty of spirit*.

What we have here, in the Beatitudes, are the steps of living the life of a Christ-follower. Don't know where to begin in your walk with Jesus? Start here. Start with *mourning* because you are truly *poor in spirit*, as are we all, and go from there, asking God and considering how to recognize each point and how to apply it in your daily life.

And what is our reward when we have 'climbed' this mountain of the Beatitudes and become ever so 'holy' and 'saintly'?

> *Blessed are you when people insult you, persecute you and falsely say all kinds of evil against you because of me. Rejoice and be glad, because great is your reward in heaven, for in the same way they persecuted the prophets*

who were before you.

This, then, is where the text turns itself around and looks to your future because you have dealt with the past and present in the previous verses.

Rejoice and be glad!, you who are persecuted for Christ's sake, for great is your reward in heaven! Those who have come to the point of persecution via the *narrow way*, Christ's way, rejoice and be glad! You share in Christ's death, you will share in Christ's everlasting life!

> *For God so loved the world that he gave his one and only Son, that whoever believes in him shall not perish but have eternal life. –John 3:16*

Yes!!! ... Ya! ... Well, I mean... Er...

Yes, this is as hard as understanding '*blessed are those who mourn*'. I don't pretend to think that ending on an vacuous note of heart-pumping enthusiasm does justice to the actual day-in-and-day-out life of a struggling Christ-follower.

Christ was headed to the cross. We are headed to suffering for His sake. We are not Christ, we are not God, we're just people, and we don't have what it takes like He did...

> *Now I rejoice in what I am suffering for you, and I fill up in my flesh what is still lacking in regard to Christ's afflictions, for the sake of his body, which is the church. I have become its servant by the commission God gave*

*me to present to you the word of God in its fullness—
the mystery that has been kept hidden for ages and
generations, but is now disclosed to the Lord's people.* **To
them God has chosen to make known among the Gentiles
the glorious riches of this mystery, which is Christ in you,
the hope of glory.**

*He is the one we proclaim, admonishing and teaching ev-
eryone with all wisdom, so that we may present everyone
fully mature in Christ. To this end I strenuously contend
with all the energy Christ so powerfully works in me.*

-Collosians 1:24-29

**Christ is *in you*, Christian, your *hope of glory!* You can because
He is able and He is with you.**

*The Lord is my strength and my defense; he has become
my salvation. He is my God, and I will praise him, my
father's God, and I will exalt him. -Exodus 15:2*

Selah.

*Author's Note[11]: I realize now, long after I wrote this piece, that
ending on this statement lacks "how" value: What does it actually
mean, "Christ is in you?" I have a written another piece that I feel
complements this one and follows up on the conclusion, "Christ in
you, the hope of glory," – Be perfect as your Heavenly Father is
perfect – Wait, what? [Included in this book] I hope it helps follow
this thought, makes it clearer, and maybe makes it more practical.*

10

Be perfect as your Heavenly Father is perfect – Wait, what?

When you read Jesus's words, "Be perfect, therefore, as your heavenly Father is perfect," (Matthew 5:48) it's all too easy to wonder for a brief moment how that could be, and then go about your day, forgetful of the awkward sense of impossibility you felt, until the next time you read or hear that verse. But it's always there, haunting the back of your mind: *God demands perfection! That's not me! What sacrifice is left for me?*

There's good news, of course, in the context, in the original language, and in the realization that, as a famous pastor once said: God has made no provision for you to live the Christian life in your own strength, intelligence, or ability – *it's better than that!*

In context, love both friend and enemy.

The first place to start when studying a verse is the immediate context. In this case, the common heading for this section is "Love Your Enemies,"

> *You have heard that it was said, 'Love your neighbor and hate your enemy.' But I tell you, love your enemies and pray for those who persecute you, that you may be children of your Father in heaven.*
>
> *He causes his sun to rise on the evil and the good, and sends rain on the righteous and the unrighteous.*
>
> *If you love those who love you, what reward will you get? Are not even the tax collectors doing that? And if you greet only your own people, what are you doing more than others? Do not even pagans do that?*
>
> *Be perfect, therefore, as your heavenly Father is perfect.*
>
> *–Matthew 5:43–48*

In a helpful Hermeneutics Stack Exchange answer[12], the author concisely lays out for us that just as God shows (acts out) love towards both those who are evil and those who are good–"*He causes his sun to rise on the evil and the good, and sends rain on the righteous and the unrighteous*"–we too must love both friend and enemy, if we want to follow God.

The context reveals to us that the way in which we are to be perfect is to love one another.

The same Stack Exchange answer mentioned above also answers the objections that it is overreaching to equate "perfection" with "love," and quotes Romans, Galatians, James, and John, in support showing this is how the apostles understood love.

The Greek of Perfection

It's helpful at this point to look at the original language, Greek[13], in surviving manuscripts, for the word translated "perfect". We are tempted to read the word "perfect" or "perfection" in personal terms, when reading Jesus's teachings to us, and in all-encompassing terms in relation to our characteristics and abilities. We are not perfect, we know that, and we also know we, at our absolute best, will never, ever, be perfect. That's about the moment it begins to feel awkward having Jesus tell us, 'be perfect as I am perfect.'

BibleHub.com is a great tool to easily look up words in the original language. Check out Matthew 5:48 on Bible Hub, then click Greek near the top-middle of the screen to view the Greek words in a table, then click the Greek word for "perfect," τέλειοι (teleioi), to view a list of verses in the bible that use the same Greek word and how they are translated in English there. You'll see translations of the Greek word such as *be mature, be men, be full grown [in your thinking],* and of course, *perfect, entire, complete,* etc.

In this sense, it helps me to understand what Jesus is saying is not simply 'I must think/act/be perfect,' as if I were able in my own abilities, but 'I must fully understand love' or 'I must be complete in who I love.' This helps us get away from focusing on our clear and obvious failings.

Oh, one more thing, you must think, act, and actually be perfect.

Didn't I *just* say it's not about being perfect? Ya, sort of, -ish, not really, though, because what I said was it's "not simply" about thinking, acting, and being perfect. As Jesus said, *"unless your righteousness surpasses that of the Pharisees and the teachers of the law, you will certainly not enter the kingdom of heaven."* (Matthew 5:20) This is when my mind reaches for that exasperated response of the Apostles, 'Who then can be saved??' (Luke 18:26; very out of context here but the exasperation is apt).

Now, the Pharisees were the *ultra-perfect* of the day. They kept the Law and they let everyone know it. Note how Jesus words it, though, *"unless your righteousness <u>surpasses</u> that of the pharisees and the teachers of the law, you will certainly not enter the kingdom of heaven."* Ack! Who then can be saved?!

Seriously, Jesus seems to be saying contradictory things here. We must be perfect as our Heavenly Father is perfect and the Pharisees aren't even perfect enough.

How does this even work?

One hint lies in the context where Jesus said those words,

> *Do not think that I have come to abolish the Law or the Prophets; I have not come to abolish them but to fulfill them. For truly I tell you, until heaven and earth disappear, not the smallest letter, not the least stroke of a pen, will by any means disappear from the Law until everything is accomplished. -Matthew 5:17-18*

The hint is there when Jesus said *"I have not come to abolish them but to fulfill them."* The Law brought righteousness to those who could keep the Law. Nobody could keep the Law. Nobody was righteous: *"We all, like sheep, have gone astray..."* (Isaiah 53:6).

But then Jesus, who *is* God and *is* righteous, came and kept the Law. He needed no sacrifice for sins.

So, when He hung and died on the cross, doing His Father's Will, He was the *"Lamb of God, who takes away the sin of the world!"* (John 1:29) Jesus was *our* sacrifice for *our* sins, and when God sees Jesus's blood, attributed to those who believe Jesus is their only hope before the Heavenly Father, God passes over us.

> *On that same night I will pass through Egypt and strike down every firstborn of both people and animals, and I will bring judgment on all the gods of Egypt. I am the Lord. ^{13} The blood will be a sign for you on the houses where you are, and **when I see the blood, I will pass over you.** No destructive plague will touch you when I strike*

Egypt. –Exodus 12:12–13

Selah. Pause, and calmly think on that. Jesus is our righteousness. Jesus is our *perfection.*

But, where is my righteousness now?

Jesus may have been our righteousness through His sacrifice on the cross but that happened a long time ago. Jesus ascended to Heaven. Where is my perfection now? I certainly don't feel it.

This is the mystery God spoke from the beginning, revealed to you, and of which Paul said of the Holy Spirit given us after Jesus ascended,

> The mystery that has been kept hidden for ages and generations, but is now disclosed to the Lord's people. To them God has chosen to make known among the Gentiles the glorious riches of this mystery, which is Christ in you, the hope of glory. –Colossians 1:26–27

Straight up awesome.

Be perfect as your Heavenly Father is perfect – Jesus is my perfection.

To this day, whenever I hear those words, "be perfect as your Heavenly Father is perfect," I cringe a little bit. I have to process in my mind what it's really saying. Then I have to remember what Jesus was really saying during the sermon on the mount.

Then I remember the truth.

God sees the blood, Jesus's blood on the cross, and He passes over me, and I enter the Kingdom of Heaven, because I am perfect as my Heavenly Father is perfect, because **Jesus is my perfection**.

Selah.

11

The End is Near: Seeing the Kingdom that is near, here, within, and coming.

I was struck by an idea presented in a recent church service: The Kingdom of Heaven is more than meets the eye: The Kingdom of Heaven has come *near* you, it is *here*, it is *within* you, and the Kingdom of Heaven is *coming.* We tend to think the Kingdom of Heaven as something in the future that we're all waiting for, and that's true, in part, but it also carries other profound dimensions.

> *The phrases* Kingdom of Heaven *and* Kingdom of God *refer to the same thing. Jesus used both phrases one right after the other in Matthew 19:23-24, explaining to His disciples how difficult it was for people to enter the Kingdom of God/Heaven.*

The End is Near

When Jesus sent out the disciples ahead of Him to the places He would soon visit, he told them, *"When you enter a town and are welcomed, eat what is offered to you. Heal the sick who are there and tell them, 'The kingdom of God has come near to you.'"* (Luke 10:8-9)

Jesus had been teaching His disciples about the kingdom of Heaven and now the disciples were preparing the people to hear about it, as well.

You and I are those people and God has sent out his disciples to reach us. Will we welcome his servants? Or, will we reject them and have it said against us,

> *Say, 'Even the dust of your town we wipe from our feet as a warning to you. Yet be sure of this: The kingdom of God has come near.' I tell you, it will be more bearable on that day for Sodom than for that town. -Luke 10:10-11*

The End is Here

The Kingdom of Heaven is *here*, that is, Jesus ushers in the Kingdom, as he tells the pharisees, *"The coming of the kingdom of God is not something that can be observed, nor will people say, 'Here it is,' or 'There it is,' because the kingdom of God is in your midst."* (Luke 17:20-21)

God became man. God was *in your midst.* God had already begun building the Kingdom of Heaven with His disciples and followers.

When Jesus ascended to Heaven after the crucifixion, He warned His disciples, *"Do not leave Jerusalem, but wait for the gift my Father promised, which you have heard me speak about. For John baptized with water, but in a few days you will be baptized with the Holy Spirit."* (Act 1:4-5)

This Holy Spirit is with you today, if you repent of your sins and follow Christ. Just as Jesus was on earth, and actually present with the disciples, the Holy Spirit is with us, and He works in us to bring forth the Kingdom of Heaven.

How?

The End is Within

I came across a very cool connection to this line of thought while researching this post and it comes from the Lord's Prayer,

Our Father in heaven, hallowed be your name, **your kingdom come, your will be done, on earth as it is in heaven.** *Give us today our daily bread. And forgive us our debts, as we also have forgiven our debtors. And lead us not into temptation, but deliver us from the evil one. -Matthew 6:9-13*

"Your kingdom come, your will be done, on earth as it is in heaven." Implied in this is that God's Kingdom is, of course, where His will would be done (just like it is in heaven), and where is a *will* done? In your heart.

[The] mystery that has been kept hidden for ages and generations, but is now disclosed to the Lord's people. To them God has chosen to make known among the Gentiles the glorious riches of this mystery, **which is Christ in you, the hope of glory.** *–Colossians 1:26–27*

The Holy Spirit, one of and one with the Trinity, Father and Son and Holy Spirit, this Holy Spirit, Christ in you, fills the heart of you if you repent and follow Jesus. By His Power, the Kingdom of Heaven is worked out from within us. The Kingdom of Heaven is within you.

The End is Coming

As alluded to earlier, the Kingdom of Heaven is wherever the King reigns, and wherever the King reigns is wherever His will is done. Jesus, on speaking of the destruction of the temple, with His disciples, said, *"And this gospel of the kingdom will be preached in the whole world as a testimony to all nations, and then the end will come."* (Matthew 24:13)

Jesus continuing to tell his disciples of the Kingdom of Heaven, made a number of comparisons: Bridesmaids waiting for the Bridegroom, servants receiving money to make a profit with while their master is away, and a comparison between sheep (believers; who do the King's Will) and goats (non-believers; who do not do the King's will) (Matthew 25). All of these parables described people waiting on a coming, which Jesus uses to point to the coming of the Kingdom of Heaven.

Finally, He says, *"For as lightning that comes from the east is visible even in the west, so will be the coming of the Son of Man."* (Matthew 24:27) We wait upon that day: The Kingdom is *coming*. One day, the end will be here.

The End is Here

If you have yet to believe, the end is near for you: Jesus has come to show us the Kingdom of Heaven. Servants of God are all about you reminding you of the Kingdom of Heaven, just like those towns to whom Jesus sent the disciples and told them to say, *'The kingdom of God has come near to you.'*

Seek the Lord while he may be found;
call on him while he is near.
Let the wicked forsake their ways
and the unrighteous their thoughts.
Let them turn to the Lord, and he will have mercy on them,
and to our God, for he will freely pardon.
–Isaiah 55:6–6

For those who believe already, the end is here. You have the Holy Spirit, 'Christ in you, the hope of glory.' You *are* the disciples sent, and being continually sent, to those towns, but for you the Kingdom of Heaven (where God's Will is done) is carried about in your body, because you are filled with the Holy Spirit. You bring and express the Kingdom of Heaven here and now insomuch as the Holy Spirit lives through you.

You are the Kingdom of Heaven in word and deed and you are a forerunner of the Kingdom of Heaven, in presence and form, when Christ returns.

Therefore, since we are surrounded by such a great cloud of witnesses, let us throw off everything that hinders and the sin that so easily entangles. And let us run with perseverance the race marked out for us, fixing our eyes on Jesus, the pioneer and perfecter of faith. For the joy set before him he endured the cross, scorning its shame, and sat down at the right hand of the throne of God. Consider him who endured such opposition from sinners, so that you will not grow weary and lose heart. -Hebrews 12:1-3

Selah.

12

Revelation

This cup is the new covenant in my blood,
which is poured out for you.
-Luke 22:20b

Circumstances of fallen heroes, failing institutions, and flawed reasoning lead me to a place of re-evaluating my faith: Welcome to deconstruction. If that doesn't sound like it deserves all the drama you'd think, you'd be right.

Deconstruction, while connected to Postmodernism (which is a whole can of worms, itself), really boils down to revisiting assumptions. And if that doesn't sound as glamorous as you'd think, from all the noise you hear about Postmodernism, you'd be right, again.

Psychology has long known and taught that our minds are dynamic and that we learn and grow over time as we gain context from experience. This continual process of growth involves a symbolic death and rebirth pattern. By experiencing regular 'little deaths', you avoid the 'Big Death'[14].

If this sounds 'new agey' to you, I promise it's not. God designed you to confront and conquer challenges, to adapt and overcome, to succeed, to transcend.

You know this symbolic death and rebirth pattern is true by your personal relationships in those times when you didn't deal with problems when they were small: You let them grow and, when it finally came time to deal with it, it was worse than it needed to be, and you felt terrible.

Deconstruction is really just the 'death' part of a healthy, continual renewal process. The upside is that this little death leads to a little rebirth, something you can handle. In other words, a renewal.

> **Do not conform to the pattern of this world, but be transformed by the renewing of your mind.** *Then you will be able to test and approve what God's will is—his good, pleasing and perfect will.* -Romans 12:2

Notice it says 'be transformed by the *renewing* of your mind' not '*renewal* of your mind'. It's continual. This 'renewing' is a pattern that you can repeat continuously, even if it is a little uncomfortable, because it is better than the alternative of a death you can't recover from.

> *There is a way that **seems right** to a man, **but its end is the way to death**. -Proverbs 14:12*

But this is a story of rebirth, reconstruction, part of healthy, continual renewal. As Christians, we are gifted with great wisdom that teaches us how to go about this.

> *Therefore, my dear friends, as you have always obeyed—not only in my presence, but now much more in my absence—***continue to work out your salvation with fear and trembling, for it is God who works in you to will and to act in order to fulfill his good purpose.***
> *–Philippians 2:12–13*

As we reach the final chapters, we'll continue to 'work out our salvation with fear and trembling', with humility, and with an eye on the mark, an eye trained on God and what He has been telling us from the start.

**This cup is the new covenant in my blood,
which is poured out for you.
-Luke 22:20b**

13

Unhitched: Inception

Ah, but a man's reach should exceed his grasp,
Or what's a heaven for?
–Robert Browning, *Andrea del Sarto*

In 2018, Pastor Andy Stanley, son of the famous pastor Charles Stanley, presented a 3-part sermon series titled "Aftermath" that became infamous for certain assertions that many thought sounded heretical.

Church leaders unhitched the church from the worldview, value system, and regulations of the Jewish Scriptures.
–Andy Stanley (Aftermath Part 3 33:21)

Since that series aired, there have been many, many who have covered, discussed, or responded to Andy and this particular series. Most have deemed it simply heretical and nothing of value was lost by letting it pass.

Despite all this, I have always thought Stanley was onto a certain something, a hint of a something about our faith, our morality, and our freedom in Christ, even if his surface ideas appear radical. I think perhaps he is 'hard to understand', as Peter would say about some of Paul's teachings.

I will not, simply, be arguing against Stanley.

What I will be doing is latching onto one particular truth and investigating it towards an end I think is perplexing, profound, and paradigm shifting.

The ideas raised and the ramifications that result are intense and long-held beliefs are questioned all over again: Questions of what's right and wrong? What's moral and immoral? Do we still follow the Ten Commandments? Do we follow the Greatest Commandment? How deep does this rabbit hole really go?

All of the ideas and questions are raised by and summed up in Jesus' words,

> ***This cup is the new covenant in my blood,***
> ***which is poured out for you.***
> ***-Luke 22:20b***

The Sermons

If you haven't listened to the sermons, already, it might be a good idea to listen to them now, at least the first part, before continuing here, so that you will have some context for what I'm launching off from.

- Aftermath, Part 1: Stand Alone[15]
- Aftermath, Part 2: Mix 'n Match[16]
- Aftermath, Part 3: Not Difficult[17]

The "Unhitch" idea

> **Peter, James, and Paul elected to unhitch the Christian faith from their Jewish scriptures, and my friends, we must as well.** And I'll tell you why. It's actually the same reason they did: **because we must not make it difficult** for those Gentiles who are turning to God. They didn't. We shouldn't either. –Andy Stanley (Aftermath Part 3 37:52)

The context of the 'unhitch' controversy is a series of sermons in which Stanley is primarily making the case that "we must not make it difficult for those Gentiles who are turning to God".

In *Aftermath Part 1*, he introduces the idea of distilling the nature of the Christian faith down to an "event" instead of a "book". Stanley does this, it seems, in the hope of evading the questions and arguments of our modern times. Things like an 'evil and maniacal God', the problem of evolution for the biblical creation narrative, problematic traditional values, and more. By focusing on the *event*, Jesus's Incarnation and Resurrection, Stanley believes he won't have to address skeptics' questions about the *book*.

> The foundation of your faith and mine is not a book. It is an event. –Andy Stanley (Aftermath Part 1 31:23)

In *Aftermath Part 2*, he builds the case that the first century church, including the Apostles, themselves, were shown by God that they should not treat Gentiles (non-Jews) as inferior: That they should not put up roadblocks to the Gentiles believing in Jesus. The Apostles are shown that they must meet with Gentiles face-to-face and they are even shown that the Gentiles receive the same Holy Spirit – yet they were not even circumcised (ie. following the Law of Moses) like the Jews. Stanley ends the scripture portion of Part 2 by presenting the dilemma of what to teach Gentiles who receive the Holy Spirit without even following the Law of Moses. He also leaves off with the very clear message that while the Old Testament (Old Covenant) is "unlivable" the New Testament (New Covenant) is "irresistible".

> *It's two fabulous covenants... and when you mix and match you get the worst of both – you'll never get the best of either. -Andy Stanley (Aftermath Part 2 32:21)*

In *Aftermath Part 3*, Stanley begins by introducing the three covenants (*Individual* – Abraham, *Nation* – Jews, *Nations* – Jews and Gentiles) and his belief how the ideas around the various covenants are contributing to many people losing their faith in modern times. He continues with the controversy of the very early church about which covenant, or which parts, the Gentiles must uphold. James and Peter declare that the Gentiles of Antioch should be held only to abstain from idols, sexual immorality, from eating things strangled, and from eating blood. Stanley argues that these were selected to make the peace and ensure unity between Jewish Christians and Gentile Christians and not to create a new Law for Gentiles. It was a little bit of give-and-take on either side, Stanley says, and not intended as a new set of rules like the Law of Moses.

> *The Old Testament, or the Law of the Prophets as they called it, was not going to be the source for any behavior in the Church. –Andy Stanley (Aftermath Part 3 31:38)*

Stanley concludes with his motivation citing James on the matter James and Peter talked about regarding requiring or not requiring the Christians of Antioch to follow Jewish customs:

> *It is my judgment, therefore, that **we should not make it difficult for the Gentiles** who are turning to God. –Acts 15:19*

Is Stanley on to something?

Did the Apostles really 'unhitch' and deny that the Old Testament Law would be the "source for any behavior in the Church"?

I will not be pointing out something new or novel about Stanley's sermons. Stanley said it bluntly, *"You are **not** accountable to the Ten Commandments. You are **not** accountable to the Jewish Law."*

> *Now, to make this point...I was going to put a screen up here: "In other words, that means thou shalt not obey the ten commandments." But I want you to hear me say it. Here's what the Jerusalem council was saying to the Gentiles: **You are not accountable to the Ten Commandments. You are not accountable to the Jewish Law. We're done with that. God has done something new.** –Andy Stanley (Aftermath Part 3 31:48)*

Is this actually true?

If it is true, what does it mean? What does it mean for how we act and behave? How we make decisions and moral choices? Things like telling the truth, or stealing, or killing?

If it's not true then we can stop right here and go back to living according to the Ten Commandments and the Great Commission and call it a day.

But, if it is true...

Then both apprehensive alarm and welcome wonder, and both at the same time, are natural responses.

Alarm because quite likely you grew up to obey the Ten Commandments, as did I, and every Christian must be alert for wolves in sheep's clothing so that we do not fall into immoral living.

Wonder, too, at the possibilities of paradigm-altering significance that part of you hesitates to believe while part of you hopes that it might have been God's plan all along.

So, is it true?

How does it play out in real life? What *are* the new rules? What's moral and immoral anymore? What's right and wrong anymore? What does the New Testament really say about the Old Testament?

Again, it's not my intention to argue for or against Stanley's Aftermath series.

My aim is to highlight something I believe Stanley has hit on that modern Christianity has forgotten or at least under-emphasized, in my estimation.

Perhaps Stanley knew what he was on to or perhaps he didn't. Maybe he had to craft a listener-friendly sermon that hindered its clarity. Whatever it was, I believe Stanley was perilously close to a truth that has ramifications for the moral paradoxes of every age.

Find out where this all leads in the second part of this series, *Unhitched: Direction.*

> ***This cup is the new covenant in my blood,***
> ***which is poured out for you.***
> *-Luke 22:20b*

14

Unhitched: Direction

Ah, but a man's reach should exceed his grasp,
Or what's a heaven for?
-Robert Browning, *Andrea del Sarto*

Andy Stanley's now infamous 2018 Aftermath series ignited a controversy over the role of the Bible, the Old Testament (Old Covenant), the New Testament (New Covenant), and our place among their teachings.

In *Unhitched: Inception*, I revisited his sermon series and refreshed our memories on what he was trying to get across.

We left off last time asking if what Stanley was saying was true. That's where we're headed next.

> *Now, to make this point...I was going to put a screen up here: "In other words, that means thou shalt not obey the ten commandments." But I want you to hear me*

say it. Here's what the Jerusalem council was saying to the Gentiles: **You are not accountable to the Ten Commandments. You are not accountable to the Jewish Law. We're done with that. God has done something new.** *–Andy Stanley (Aftermath Part 3 31:48)*

So, is it true?

Yes.

Yes, *what*?

Yes, we are not *accountable* to the Ten Commandments or the Jewish Law.

You are *accountable* to God.

And that means accountable to Christ as He is your representative in God's presence, our 'high priest forever'.

For God so loved the world that he gave his one and only Son **that whoever believes in him** *shall not perish but have eternal life. –John 3:16*

I have the power to give it up and the power to receive it back again, just as my Father commanded me to do. –John 10:18

So Christ has now become the High Priest *over all the good things that have come. He has entered that greater, more perfect Tabernacle in heaven... With his own blood...*

he entered the Most Holy Place once for all time and secured our redemption forever. -Hebrews 9:11-12

Therefore He is able to save completely those who draw near to God through Him, since **He always lives to intercede for them.** -Hebrews 7:25

Then what does 'accountable to Christ' mean? In everyday life, if we are accountable to anyone, it means we do what they tell us to do and uphold what they have told us to uphold.

As the Father has loved me, so have I loved you. Now remain in my love. **If you keep my commands, you will remain in my love, just as I have kept my Father's commands and remain in his love.** *I have told you this so that my joy may be in you and that your joy may be complete. My command is this: Love each other as I have loved you. Greater love has no one than this: to lay down one's life for one's friends.* **You are my friends if you do what I command.** -John 15:9-14

Do not think that I have come to abolish the Law or the Prophets; *I have not come to abolish them* **but to fulfill them.** *For truly I tell you, until heaven and earth disappear, not the smallest letter, not the least stroke of a pen, will by any means disappear from the Law until everything is accomplished.* -Matthew 5:17-18

Therefore anyone who sets aside one of the least of these commands and teaches others accordingly will be called least in the kingdom of heaven, but whoever practices and teaches these commands will be called great in the kingdom of heaven. –Matthew 5:19

Remember, we are not *accountable* to the Law and the Prophets: We are *accountable* to Christ. In being accountable to Christ, believing that He is the Son of God and that He was the final sacrifice for our sin, and following His commands, we *fulfill* the Law and the Prophets *through* Christ.

We don't fulfill the Law and Prophets: **Jesus** fulfills the Law and the Prophets.

It's a C.S Lewis deeper magic kind of thing.

I'm still confused. Jesus says practice and teach the Law and the Prophets.

Ah, now we're getting to it. First, we must look at Jesus' response when asked what the greatest commandment was:

One of them, an expert in the law, tested him with this question: "Teacher, which is the greatest commandment in the Law?"

*Jesus replied: "'**Love the Lord your God** with all your heart and with all your soul and with all your mind.' This is the first and greatest commandment. And the second is like it: '**Love your neighbor as yourself.' All the Law and the Prophets hang on these two commandments.**"*

–Matthew 22:37-40

Think about the last sentence for a bit: **"All the Law and the Prophets hang on these two commandments."**

It is not saying that they *replace* the Law. Jesus already said he hadn't come to abolish the Law but to fulfill the Law.

What Jesus is saying is that if you do love God and your neighbor, *truly*, you will be fulfilling the Law and the Prophets, by and through Jesus because *Jesus* fulfills the Law and the Prophets.

> ***Do not think that I have come to abolish the Law or the Prophets;*** *I have not come to abolish them* **but to fulfill them.** *-Matthew 5:17*

All the Law?

You're a quick one, aren't you. There are the Ten Commandments and then there are 600+ additional laws involving mostly civil, dietary, cleanliness, and other requirements. Will I really be upholding all of them?

Firstly, you can't uphold any of it in your sin but Jesus in His power, His redemptive work by salvation on the cross, and His resurrection and everlasting Priesthood, fulfills it for you.

Furthermore, we must understand the Law and the Prophets were given to the Jewish nation, Israel, very specifically and particularly, in covenant fashion, and not to the Gentiles (non-Jews). That is first and foremost why, for example, while we follow the Ten Commandments, because we find value in them, non-Jews do not wholly follow the rest of the Law: That is, they were not given to us.

> *Then Moses went up to God, and the Lord called to him from the mountain and said, "This is what you are to say to the descendants of Jacob and what you are to tell the people of Israel: 'You yourselves have seen what I did to Egypt, and how I carried you on eagles' wings and brought you to myself.* **Now if you obey me fully and keep my covenant, then out of all nations you will be my treasured possession.** *Although the whole earth is mine,* **you will be for me a kingdom of priests and a holy nation.***' These are the words you are to speak to the Israelites." –Exodus 19:3-6*

The 19th chapter of Exodus, quoted above, immediately precedes the Ten Commandments, given in Exodus 20, and many other laws in the following chapters.

So, then, why do we still follow the Ten Commandments? The most fundamental reason is because they are, basically, universally acknowledged as one of the best, most complete, and most concise moral codes ever followed by humans, surpassed only by the Greatest Commandment, given by Jesus, to love God and neighbor, which itself is in reference to the Law and the Ten Commandments.

We also follow the Ten Commandments because we observe a distinct and categorical difference between them and many other Old Covenant laws: The Ten Commandments deal with morality where many of the other laws deal with civil, dietary, cleanliness or other issues.

Some of the other laws do actually deal with morality like treating foreigners well and loving your neighbor. Leviticus 19, as well as many chapters throughout Leviticus, mix moral, civil, dietary, cleanliness, and other laws.

> *When a foreigner resides among you in your land, do not mistreat them.* ***The foreigner residing among you must be treated as your native-born. Love them as yourself, for you were foreigners in Egypt.*** *I am the Lord your God.*
> *–Leviticus 19:34*

The Law and the Prophets were given to the Jewish nation for a specific covenant, for a specific purpose, for a specific period (until the Old Covenant prophecies were fulfilled in Christ), and the Law was given to separate out a people for God and make them Holy (separate, sanctified) until that time.

> *Why, then, was the law given at all? It was added because of transgressions* ***until the Seed to whom the promise referred had come.*** *–Galatians 3:19a*

> *I am the Lord your God;* ***consecrate yourselves and be holy, because I am holy.*** *Do not make yourselves unclean by any creature that moves along the ground. I am the Lord, who brought you up out of Egypt to be your God; therefore be holy, because I am holy. –Leviticus 19:44–45*

> *You must therefore make a distinction between clean and unclean animals and between unclean and clean birds. Do not defile yourselves by any animal or bird or anything that moves along the ground—those that I have set apart*

as unclean for you. **You are to be holy to me because I, the Lord, am holy, and I have set you apart from the nations to be my own.** *–Leviticus 20:25–26*

Non-Jews are not under the Old Covenant of any of this, including the Ten Commandments, but we are under the New Covenant in Christ. We follow the moral laws because we follow the *greatest* moral law: The Greatest Commandment, to love God and neighbor.

So, yes, we uphold the Law and the Prophets through Jesus by following the Greatest Commandment because Jesus, Himself, fulfills the whole Law and the Prophets *for us* if we remain in Him.

As the Father has loved me, so have I loved you. Now remain in my love. **If you keep my commands, you will remain in my love, just as I have kept my Father's commands and remain in his love.** *–John 15:9–10*

Okay, it sounds true. But what does it all mean?

Here's where it gets real. Real alarming and real liberating.

Here's what the Jerusalem Council was saying to the Gentiles: You are not accountable to the Ten Commandments. You're not accountable to the Jewish law. We're done with that. God has done something new. Besides, he [Paul] would say to them and he would say to you, **thou shalt not obey the Ten Commandments because those are not your commandments. Yours are better. And yours are**

far less complicated, but they are far more demanding.
-Andy Stanley (Aftermath Part 3 31:48)

You're in uncharted territory now. Gone is the familiar and hammered-home order of a Ten Commandments-based morality you thought was the be-all-and-end-all. Now, you're left in the chaos of an unfamiliar and glossed-over *love God and neighbor* world.

With order comes the confidence of the known but also the constraints of the limits. With chaos comes the fear of the unknown but also the freedom of the possibilities.

> To the Jews who had believed him, Jesus said, **"If you hold to my teaching, you are really my disciples. Then you will know the truth, and the truth will set you free."**
>
> They answered him, "We are Abraham's descendants and have never been slaves of anyone. How can you say that we shall be set free?"
>
> Jesus replied, "Very truly I tell you, everyone who sins is a slave to sin. Now a slave has no permanent place in the family, but a son belongs to it forever. **So if the Son sets you free, you will be free indeed."**
>
> -John 8:31-36

Here in John 8, Jesus is talking to the "Jews **who had believed him**" who were still clinging to their Abrahamic, Old Covenant heritage, which included Moses, the Law, and the Prophets, while professing to believe Jesus. Jesus was introducing the New Covenant to them but they were having a hard time with it. They were in the chaos but they were also in the space of possibilities.

Jesus is telling them that they are sinners and therefore slaves in what they thought was their own family under Abraham (Old Covenant). And slaves have no permanent place. He's telling them that they are lost following the Old Covenant.

But Jesus is also telling them that a son can set a slave free: And if *the* Son sets you free, you are no longer a slave to sin (the Old Covenant), and now you have a permanent place in the true Family (the New Covenant).

> *Jesus said,* **"If you hold to my teaching, you are really my disciples.** *Then you will know the truth, and the truth will set you free." -John 8:31b*

Forgive a momentary paraphrase, if you would, but it might be helpful to switch out the word "truth" for the word "Son" just as an exercise to highlight what Jesus would say Himself in the next few verses ("So if the Son sets you free, you will be free indeed."):

Jesus said, "If you hold to my teaching, you are really my disciples. **Then you will know the *Son*, and the *Son* will set you free."** (John 8:31b)

Navigating Liberation

So maybe we are 'unhitched' from the Old Testament. Maybe we do a have a better and more demanding set of commandments. Where do we go from here? How do we decide what's right and wrong in everyday life if Jesus' teachings are now the standard?

The Ten Commandments say "don't kill", so what do we do about war? The Ten Commandments say "don't give false testimony", so what do we do about lying to those wanting to harm us or others? The Ten Commandments say "Keep the Sabbath Day" but what about the Gentiles who don't have the Jewish Sabbath? The Ten Commandments say "honor your parents" but what if honoring your parents looks to others like dis-honoring them?

We're finally going to get into how the New Covenant in Jesus gives us the wisdom to navigate these questions in *Unhitched: Liberation.*

This cup is the new covenant in my blood,
which is poured out for you.
-Luke 22:20b

15

Unhitched: Liberation

Ah, but a man's reach should exceed his grasp,
Or what's a heaven for?
–Robert Browning, *Andrea del Sarto*

Andy Stanley's Aftermath series ignited a controversy over the role of the Old Testament (Old Covenant) and the New Testament (New Covenant) in the way that Christians live.

In *Unhitched: Inception*, I revisited his sermon series and refreshed our memories on what he was trying to get across. In *Unhitched: Direction*, I laid out the biblical case for the way in which Stanley was right.

In the last part, we admitted maybe we are unhitched from the Old Covenant and that maybe we do have a better and more demanding set of commandments in the New Covenant in Jesus' blood instead of the Old Covenant Law and Prophets.

But where are we supposed to go from there? By 'unhitching' we're now outside the order and confidence we felt with the boundaries of the Old Covenant and instead we're placed in the unboundaried chaos of the unknown in a *love God and neighbor* world.

Well, what's a Heaven for, anyway? Let's see where such a world takes us.

The Greatest Commandment

Jesus told us the Greatest Commandment is to love God and neighbor.

> *Jesus replied: "'**Love the Lord your God** with all your heart and with all your soul and with all your mind.' This is the first and greatest commandment. And the second is like it: '**Love your neighbor** as yourself.' All the Law and the Prophets hang on these two commandments."*
> *-Matthew 22:37-38*

Love God

What does it mean to Love God? As we talked about with Jesus, it at least means valuing and upholding what God values and upholds.

God is a relational being, He has revealed Himself to us, and communicated with us. Such a being is capable of love and desiring love. God tells us and shows us that He loves us and the God revealed to us is worthy of love in return.

*Long ago the LORD said to Israel: "I have loved you, my
people, with an everlasting love. With unfailing love I
have drawn you to myself." -Jeremiah 31:3*

God tells us through His servants, the Prophets, that we should
love Him with all that we are.

*Hear, O Israel: The Lord our God, the Lord is one. Love
the Lord your God with all your heart and with all your
soul and with all your strength. -Deuteronomy 6:4-5*

God has told us what to do and how to act and so, if we love Him,
then we ought to do what God has said. And what has God said?
The Ten Commandments are a good place to start.

No other gods. No idols. No misuse of God's Name.
Keep the Sabbath Day. honor your parents. No murder.
No adultery. No stealing. No perjury. No coveting. -
Exodus 20

Jesus tells us we should do the Will of God if we truly love Him,
as we love family.

*He replied to him, "Who is my mother, and who are my
brothers?" Pointing to his disciples, he said, "Here are my
mother and my brothers. For whoever does the will of my
Father in heaven is my brother and sister and mother."
-Matthew 12:48-50*

What is God's Will? The Sermon on the Mount given by Jesus
breaks it down.

Blessed are those who are poor, who mourn, who are meek, who hunger and thirst after righteousness, who are merciful, who are pure in heart, who are peacemakers, and who are persecuted because of righteousness.

Be Salt and Light. Fulfill the Law. Reconcile with your enemy. No adultery. No divorce. Keep your word. Love your enemies. Give to the needy. Live out the Lord's Prayer. God-honoring fasting. Keep your hope in heaven and not on earth. Keep yourself innocent. Do not worry.

Judge others the way you would want to be judged. Ask, seek, and knock with God and keep on asking, seeking, and knocking. Follow the narrow way that leads to life. Bear good fruit in doing the Will of God. Act on God's Words.

-Matthew 5-7

And God tells us we must not confuse material sacrifice with obedience.

But Samuel replied: "Does the LORD delight in burnt offerings and sacrifices as much as in obeying the LORD? To obey is better than sacrifice, and to heed is better than the fat of rams. -1 Samuel 15:22

The Bible has shown us that God loves us, how we are to love God in return, and what God values that He wants us to value.

In these ways, we love God.

Love Neighbor

So, we are to love God and listen to what He says. Jesus has told us to love God and neighbor. How does that play out in real life?

> *Do not seek revenge or bear a grudge against anyone among your people, but love your neighbor as yourself. I am the Lord. –Leviticus 19:18*

We are to do good without even expecting good in return.

> *But love your enemies, do good to them, and lend to them without expecting to get anything back. Then your reward will be great, and you will be children of the Most High, because he is kind to the ungrateful and wicked. –Luke 6:35*

We are even to love and pray for our enemies.

> *But I tell you, love your enemies and pray for those who persecute you, –Matthew 5:44*

And we must show love to foreigners in our land.

> *And you are to love those who are foreigners, for you yourselves were foreigners in Egypt. –Deuteronomy 10:19*

That's it?

The question I'm interested in is broader and deeper than just what commands do we follow.

So, that *would* be it if Jesus hadn't given us more direction by His own words and by the Holy Spirit through the Apostles. There is the Greatest Commandment and then Jesus gave us the Great Commission.

> *Then Jesus came to them and said, "All authority in heaven and on earth has been given to me. Therefore go and make disciples of all nations, baptizing them in the name of the Father and of the Son and of the Holy Spirit, and teaching them to obey everything I have commanded you. And surely I am with you always, to the very end of the age." -Matthew 28:18-20*

What I really want to know is more like 'what should I be doing at any given moment'? And how do I know what's right in hard situations? Situations that aren't necessarily right vs wrong, such as decisions with two or more good choices, or dilemmas with only bad choices.

For questions of what we should be doing, rather than what is right and wrong, Jesus once again distills the answer from the heart of the Greatest Commandment: If we love God then we will value what He values, the New Covenant, and if we love our neighbor then we will reach out to them and make disciples to the New Covenant, that is, to Jesus.

In these ways, we love our neighbor.

Preach the Gospel

The Great Commission lays it out simply. In the simplicity of the commission there is a distinct goal to accomplish and yet great freedom in how we are to accomplish it.

> *Then Jesus came to them and said, "All authority in heaven and on earth has been given to me. Therefore go and **make disciples of all nations**, baptizing them in the name of the Father and of the Son and of the Holy Spirit, and **teaching them to obey everything I have commanded you**. And surely I am with you always, to the very end of the age." –Matthew 28:18–20*

You are to make disciples to the Gospel, the "good news" Jesus taught us, so what does the Bible say that is?

> *For God so loved the world that he gave his one and only Son, that whoever believes in him shall not perish but have eternal life. –John 3:16*

Sometimes we over-complicate things. A million questions can come up about sharing the Gospel and we can get lost in preparing answers to the infinite number of possible questions but the Bible shows us how to focus on the Gospel.

> *The jailer called for lights, rushed in and fell trembling before Paul and Silas. He then brought them out and asked, "Sirs, what must I do to be saved?"*

*They replied, "**Believe in the Lord Jesus, and you will be saved**—you and your household." Then they spoke the word of the Lord to him and to all the others in his house.*
–Acts 16:29-32

The good news, the Gospel, is simply believing in Jesus and what He has done for us.

Questions will come up, though, so the Bible encourages us to be ready at any time to challenge and encourage others with patience.

Preach the word; be prepared in season and out of season; correct, rebuke and encourage—with great patience and careful instruction. –2 Timothy 4:2

The Bible tells us to preach the Gospel and we might be timid or feel foolish about sharing our message but we are told to be bold and confident in our message.

*For **I am not ashamed of the gospel, because it is the power of God that brings salvation to everyone who believes**: first to the Jew, then to the Gentile. –Romans 1:16*

In these ways, we preach the Gospel.

Make Disciples

Discipling is an archaic word and a lost art form but it is the core of what Christians are called by Christ to do. The Bible has many things to say about this. Discipling is the bulk of the heart of the New Testament. From Jesus and His disciples, to the Apostles and the Churches, to the Churches and their Witness, it was all to reach out and disciple new believers in the faith.

> *Go therefore and **make disciples of all the nations**, baptizing them in the name of the Father and the Son and the Holy Spirit, teaching them to observe all that I commanded you; and lo, I am with you always, even to the end of the age. -Matthew 28:19-20*

> *And the things you have heard me say in the presence of many witnesses **entrust to reliable people who will also be qualified to teach others.** -2 Timothy 2:2*

> *This is to my Father's glory, that you bear much fruit, showing yourselves to be my disciples. -John 15:8*

> *How, then, can they call on the one they have not believed in? And how can they believe in the one of whom they have not heard? And how can they hear without someone preaching to them? -Romans 10:14-15*

> *All Scripture is God-breathed and is useful for teaching, rebuking, correcting and training in righteousness, so that the servant of God may be thoroughly equipped for every good work. -2 Timothy 3:16-17*

Once you see it, you can't unsee it. The entire way in which our early faith grew was through discipling. God, again, has given us great freedom in how to go about accomplishing this but it all comes back to discipling.

In these ways, we make disciples.

Something's Missing

We've come from a new set of commandments, that frames right and wrong, to a new guide on what we should be doing but something feels off, doesn't it? Something's not quite right. Something's missing.

When the only choices are bad choices we start to feel that there are some dilemmas in life that are no-win dilemmas.

Is it wrong for someone starving to steal food?

Is it wrong to lie about planning a surprise party you're throwing?

Is it wrong to kill in war?

All these things we generally feel uncomfortable about and generally ignore so we don't have to think about it.

Yet most of us would call a lie a lie, even if we call it by a nicer name: A white lie.

A lie is a lie, isn't it? A lie is one of those moral laws we still uphold, right?

Lies will be judged.

Yes they will.

And they will be judged by *the* Judge, Jesus Christ, under the New Covenant, according to the Greatest Commandment: Love God and neighbor.

As we talked about in the last part of this series, you *will* break the Law Jesus said to "practice" and "teach" but when you break the word of the Law out of love for God and neighbor you fulfill the New Covenant and are covered by the missing piece.

Mercy Triumphs Over Judgment

> *Speak and act as those who are going to be judged by the law that gives freedom, because judgment without mercy will be shown to anyone who has not been merciful.* **Mercy triumphs over judgment.** -James 2:12-13

You can breathe a sigh of relief. The Bible has you covered.

How do you decide what is right to do in those situations of moral dilemmas?

There are many times when it arises that our moral commandments must be broken for what we innately feel is a moral virtue. These moral difficulties cause us to break a commandment no matter what choice we make.

Do you tell the truth and reveal the location of the Jews in hiding to a Nazi officer ensuring their death? Or do you lie to protect their lives? You are guilty of innocent death on one hand or you are guilty of lying on the other hand. Picking one because it seems like the lesser evil is still picking an evil, isn't it?

How do you make the choice without sinning? Do you ignore the problem because it's difficult? Do you ignore the choice and not act? Not making a choice is making a choice, isn't it? In not making a choice, have you loved God and neighbor? If not, you sin.

First, do what Jesus said to do.

> *But love your enemies, do good to them, and lend to them without expecting to get anything back. Then your reward will be great, and you will be children of the Most High, because he is kind to the ungrateful and wicked. Be merciful, just as your Father is merciful. –Luke 6:35–36*

You are loving your enemy when you do that which steers them away from sin.

Surprise! This has always been the way, even in the Old Testament. Jesus came to fulfill the Law and the Prophets, remember, not to abolish them.

> **For I desire mercy**, *not sacrifice, and acknowledgment of God rather than burnt offerings. –Hosea 6:6*

This is cool but how does 'mercy triumph over judgment',

exactly?

> *Be merciful, just as your Father is merciful. Do not judge,*
> *and **you** will not be judged. Do not condemn, and **you***
> *will not be condemned. Forgive, and **you** will be forgiven.*
> *–Luke 6:36–37*

It's **you**. **You** will receive the triumph of mercy over judgment.

> ***Speak and act as those who are going to be judged*** *by the*
> *law that gives freedom,* ***because judgment without mercy***
> ***will be shown to anyone who has not been merciful.***
> *Mercy triumphs over judgment. –James 2:12–13*

When you have to make a choice in which wrong will result, since you have done it with Love for God and your neighbor, in the spirit of protecting those people who need to hear the Gospel and become disciples, you are covered by God's mercy through Jesus Christ's atoning sacrifice on the Cross and His everlasting Priesthood by which he prays and intercedes for you continually.

> *So Christ has now become the High Priest over all the good*
> *things that have come. He has entered that greater, more*
> *perfect Tabernacle in heaven... With his own blood...**he***
> ***entered the Most Holy Place once for all time and secured***
> ***our redemption forever.*** *–Hebrews 9:11–12*

> *Therefore He is able to save completely those who draw*
> *near to God through Him, since **He always lives to***
> ***intercede for them.*** *–Hebrews 7:25*

What about those moral dilemmas?

Understanding the New Covenant reveals the truth about the simpler and more demanding commandment, the Greatest Commandment:

Love God and Neighbor

The Great Commission gives us direction in the choices of life:

Preach the Gospel and Make Disciples

And in all of this, in all of our human failing, we fall on God's mercy:

Mercy Triumphs over Judgment

Keeping these three things in mind we can answer a lot of questions about life and moral dilemmas not only intellectually but with a clear conscience before God.

Is it wrong to steal food if you're starving?

Ask the questions: Have you loved God in doing so? Have you loved your neighbor?

> *There will always be poor people in the land. There-*
> *fore I command you to* **be openhanded** *toward your*
> *fellow Israelites* **who are poor and needy** *in your land.*
> *-Deuteronomy 15:11*

*"Do not seek revenge or bear a grudge against anyone among your people, but **love your neighbor as yourself**. I am the LORD." –Leviticus 19:18*

If God, Himself, has said to be openhanded to the poor and needy, and they must resort to stealing food, then exactly who has failed to love God and their neighbor? Is it the thief? Or is it those who have no need to steal?

The poor and needy will be covered by mercy if they seek to love God and neighbor.

Is it wrong to lie about planning a surprise party you're throwing?

Ask the questions: Have you loved God in doing so? Have you loved your neighbor?

Are you loving your neighbor as yourself by blessing them in this way? Then you have loved God by upholding what God upholds and valuing what God has valued.

Is it wrong to kill in war?

You know the drill.

Ask the questions: Have you loved God in doing so? Have you loved your neighbor?

This one's harder, isn't it? How is it possible to love God or your neighbor in *killing* them?

Maybe it's not.

But maybe the way in which you are loving God is by loving the other neighbor who is also under threat.

Even in killing, one can see love in action and the moment of mercy that resistance provides to a foe to reconsider their ways and turn back from sin.

But sometimes reason fails. Sometimes moral gray areas get the best of our ability to think through them. Sometimes there's no time.

Show mercy and you will be shown mercy.

> *Speak and act as those who are going to be judged by the law that gives freedom, because judgment without mercy will be shown to anyone who has not been merciful.* **Mercy triumphs over judgment.** –James 2:12-13

What about the other laws, like adultery, sexual immorality, coveting?

Some things are still wrong. I am not suggesting a universal 'get out of jail free' card.

You know the drill. You can know if something is right or wrong by asking the questions:

Am I loving God and valuing what He values?

Am I loving my neighbor as I love myself?

You will find that if you ask these questions and *really* think them through you'll find almost all laws you might question are better served obeyed. But where loving God or loving your neighbor is more truly upheld by letting go of the Old Covenant Law then you fall upon the New Covenant mercy in Jesus' shed blood on the Cross.

You *are* breaking the Law. But you are not *accountable* to the Law. You are accountable to the New Covenant in Jesus' blood and His covenant requires you to love God and neighbor as the Greatest Commandment.

> ***This cup is the new covenant in my blood,***
> ***which is poured out for you.***
> ***–Luke 22:20b***

Simplify

Love God and Neighbor
Preach the Gospel and Make Disciples
Mercy Triumphs over Judgment

You can see how much simpler it is to think through the New Covenant's application to our everyday decisions than it is the Old Covenant and its Ten Commandments let alone its additional 600+ laws.

I would rather look at the world through a lens of a few rules than 10 or 600 any day.

But as we discussed even the Greatest Commandment refers back to the Law and the Prophets.

> **Do not think that I have come to abolish the Law or the Prophets;** *I have not come to abolish them* **but to fulfill them.** *For truly I tell you, until heaven and earth disappear, not the smallest letter, not the least stroke of a pen, will by any means disappear from the Law until everything is accomplished. -Matthew 5:17-18*

> *Therefore anyone who sets aside one of the least of these commands and teaches others accordingly will be called least in the kingdom of heaven, but whoever practices and teaches these commands will be called great in the kingdom of heaven. -Matthew 5:19*

You must learn the Law and the Prophets for yourself, because they teach you what God has said, what God values, and what God upholds. You must then apply the Law and the Prophets through the New Covenant and the Greatest Commandment.

In so doing you will keep yourself safe in the wisdom the Holy Spirit gives to us through the Bible.

> *All Scripture is God-breathed and is useful for teaching, rebuking, correcting and training in righteousness, so that the servant of God a may be thoroughly equipped for every good work. -2 Timothy 3:16-17*

> *These [Old Testament] things* **happened to them as examples and were written down as warnings for us,**

on whom the culmination of the ages has come. So, if you
think you are standing firm, be careful that you don't fall!
–1 Corinthians 10:11–12

Aftermath

Love God and Neighbor
Preach the Gospel and Make Disciples
Mercy Triumphs over Judgment

These are the New Covenant paradigms Jesus gave to us, Himself, and by the Apostles through the Holy Spirit.

These are the lens through which you can view life, your obligations to God, your requirements to your neighbor, what you are to do with your life, and, mercy, the key that makes sense of moral dilemmas.

We're going to wrap up and distill these principles into a handy and manageable form you can easily remember and carry around with you in *Unhitched: Aftermath.*

See you there.

This cup is the new covenant in my blood,
which is poured out for you.
–Luke 22:20b

16

Unhitched: Aftermath

Ah, but a man's reach should exceed his grasp,
Or what's a heaven for?
-Robert Browning, *Andrea del Sarto*

If you've made it all the way through this series riffing off Andy Stanley's controversial Aftermath sermon series then congratulations. It's been a long haul but I hope it's been worth it and I hope, just maybe, that it has been a mind-expanding journey, as it was for me.

In *Unhitched: Inception*, I revisited Stanley's Aftermath sermon series and refreshed our memories on what he was trying to get across. In *Unhitched: Direction*, I laid out the biblical case for the way in which Stanley was right. And in *Unhitched: Liberation*, I went through the principles Jesus gave us in the New Covenant and the ramifications they have for how we live our lives.

The last part ended with focusing on the simplicity of the

New Covenant and how it provides a simpler guide to life's complexity.

Today, we're going to wrap things up by focusing on the pillars of the New Covenant.

Distillation

If you remember nothing else, remember these principles given to us by the New Covenant in Jesus.

Love God and Neighbor

*Jesus replied: "'**Love the Lord your God** with all your heart and with all your soul and with all your mind.' This is the first and greatest commandment. And the second is like it: '**Love your neighbor as yourself.**' All the Law and the Prophets hang on these two commandments." –Matthew 22:37–40*

Preach the Gospel and Make Disciples

*Then Jesus came to them and said, "All authority in heaven and on earth has been given to me. Therefore go and **make disciples** of all nations, baptizing them in the name of the Father and of the Son and of the Holy Spirit, and **teaching them to obey everything I have commanded** you. And surely I am with you always, to the very end of the age." –Matthew 28:18–20*

Mercy Triumphs over Judgment

Speak and act as those who are going to be judged by the law that gives freedom, because judgment without mercy will be shown to anyone who has not been merciful. **Mercy triumphs over judgment.** –James 2:12–13

You thought there was more?

Sorry to disappoint but my wisdom ends well before the Bible's. What I've tried to do in this series is highlight something Stanley, himself, mentioned but didn't dive into as much as I think we should given its importance and relevance to how we actually live out our Christian life.

I hope I have at least sparked something in your mind by latching onto one particular truth Stanley was able to surface that I think is perplexing, profound, and paradigm-shifting:

> **This cup is the new covenant in my blood,**
> **which is poured out for you.**
> **–Luke 22:20b**

Practice it

I don't want to end without encouraging you to play these principles out in your thinking about choices you actually make in your everyday life.

Consciously and intentionally walk through choices according to these principles.

You just might find that your choices are different and the way you got there was simpler.

What's up with the Robert Browning quote?

> **Ah, but a man's reach should exceed his grasp,**
> **Or what's a heaven for?**
> **–Robert Browning, *Andrea del Sarto*[18]**

For many of us conservative Christians, we were brought up in, taught, and soaked in a moral system that intentionally or unintentionally can lead to an over-emphasis on particular rights and wrongs, down to exact wording, the letter of the Law rather than the spirit of the Law.

> *Woe to you, teachers of the law and Pharisees, you hypocrites! You give a tenth of your spices—mint, dill and cumin.* ***But you have neglected the more important matters of the law—justice, mercy and faithfulness.*** *You should have practiced the latter, without neglecting the former. You blind guides! You strain out a gnat but swallow a camel. -Matthew 23:23-24*

In writing this series, I have had to intentionally and methodically consider what is really going on with the Old and New Covenants. I have felt exactly like my reach was beyond my actual grasp. There is something deeply profound about the New Covenant. Like a "magic" deeper than the "magic" we already knew.

I suspect the ideas in this series are as unsettling to some as they were to me. I know they may *sound* heretical. I know they *sound* like they might allow for immoral living. I don't think that's the case when the New Covenant is rightly understood, though.

The freedom granted to you in the New Covenant is simpler but far more demanding.

> *Therefore, my dear friends, as you have always obeyed—not only in my presence, but now much more in my absence—***continue to work out your salvation with fear and trembling, for it is God who works in you to will and to act in order to fulfill his good purpose***. -Philippians 2:12-13*

In working out our faith, what are we doing if not trying to reach somewhere we can't reach yet, that is until 'God works in us' to discover the "more important matters of the law."

So, be brave. Give yourself a chance to reach beyond grasp and discover something new.

Besides, what's a Heaven for, anyway?

> **For God so loved the world that he gave his one and only Son that whoever believes in him shall not perish but have eternal life. -John 3:16**

> **This cup is the new covenant in my blood, which is poured out for you.**
> **-Luke 22:20b**

17

Integration

*One doesn't discover new lands without consenting
to lose sight of the shore for a very long time. -André
Gide*

**Writers will know what I mean when I say, I feel a great sense
of peace once I have gotten something out of my head and onto
the page.** Until then, certain ideas, not all, not even many, but
certain few course through one's mind, living a life of their own,
torturing the Writer's mind until he makes them permanent,
or at least more permanent than himself. If left too long, some
ideas die, forgotten. Yet, so it is with ideas that escape, that they
are birthed, saved. The immaterial made manifest in material.
Ideal made actual. Heaven brought down to earth. So the Writer
is saved.

The great irony is that this is the opposite of our expectations.
We expect to be taken up to Heaven and not Heaven brought
down to us. How could material ever adequately reflect imma-

terial? It is not right that *actual* be greater than *ideal.* How can *word* ever live up to *thought?*

Yet, at every turn, God upends the upside world we know and shows us something better, more surprising, and truer. He creates Man, made in the image of God, out of breath and dust. He creates Woman, Beauty in Person, out of a rib bone. He creates the World and then destroys it in the Flood. He builds up a Nation for Himself and then withers it in the Wilderness. He rescues a Nation from oppression and then rescues it from decadence by sending it into oppression, again. He warns against setting up kings and kingdoms and then uses a king to bring about *the* King and *the* Kingdom. He Curses Man and Creation and then manifests the Holy into that Unholy making it Holy, again. He upholds the Law and the Prophets by Fulfilling an Old Covenant with a New Covenant. He ascends into Heaven to descend to a new Jerusalem. He enters into Time to provide us a path to Eternity.

So it is with this faith that resists our attempts to tame and domesticate it. A continual renewal, reversal, and inversion.

Words escape. The page is read and the mind births ideas. The material is made manifest in the immaterial. Actual is made ideal. Earth is brought up to Heaven. So the Heart is saved.

Patterns revealed in time and space gifted to us so that we could understand something real. By them, we can piece together a picture of the whole. We can look back through the Prism of Creation, see the colors converge, the many become one, impure become pure, and diversity become unity.

As it is said, God works in mysterious ways. This was my path. Now, wherever it leads, it's part of your path, too. In truth, whether they can see it or not, can grasp it or not, this is everyone's path. This is reconstruction from deconstruction.

Love God and Neighbor
Preach the Gospel and Make Disciples
Mercy Triumphs over Judgment

This cup is the new covenant in my blood,
which is poured out for you.
–Luke 22:20b

18

One More Thing

**Revolution is simply the process of going in circles.
What the world needs now is not revolution but
redemption.**

Jesus gave His life to free you from a system of laws that was unable to and was never intended to save you in your sin.

We who are Jews by birth and not sinful Gentiles know that a person is not justified by the works of the law, but by faith in Jesus Christ. **So we, too, have put our faith in Christ Jesus that we may be justified by faith in Christ and not by the works of the law, because by the works of the law no one will be justified.**

But if, in seeking to be justified in Christ, we Jews find ourselves also among the sinners, doesn't that mean that Christ promotes sin? Absolutely not! If I rebuild what I destroyed, then I really would be a lawbreaker.

For through the law I died to the law so that I might live for God. I have been crucified with Christ and I no longer live, but Christ lives in me. The life I now live in the body, I live by faith in the Son of God, who loved me and gave himself for me. I do not set aside the grace of God, **for if righteousness could be gained through the law, Christ died for nothing!**

-Galatians 2:15-21

Jesus replied, "Very truly I tell you, everyone who sins is a slave to sin. Now a slave has no permanent place in the family, but a son belongs to it forever. **So if the Son sets you free, you will be free indeed."** *-John 8:31-36*

Jesus said, "If you hold to my teaching, you are really my disciples. **Then you will know the truth, and the truth will set you free."** *-John 8:31b*

Today, if you hear his voice, do not harden your hearts *as you did at Meribah, as you did that day at Massah in the desert, where your fathers tested and tried me, though they had seen what I did. -Hebrews 3:8*

For God so loved the world that he gave his one and only Son that whoever believes in him shall not perish but have eternal life. -John 3:16

**This cup is the new covenant in my blood,
which is poured out for you.**
-Luke 22:20b

Notes

INSPIRATION

1   The meat of this book are collected essays glued together with chapters that provide insight and context to how they all fit together and to my personal journey of deconstruction and reconstruction. You will find the essays will often have a different tone and style compared to the 'glue chapters' as the essays were written some time ago.

2   My use of "deconstruction" and "reconstruction" will be a little loose in this book. My use of *deconstruction* aligns mostly with Postmodernism. My use of *reconstruction*, on the other hand, has little resemblance to related ideas (eg. Reconstructionism, Reconstructivism, etc.). I am using the word in this book to show the opposite process to deconstruction.

PRISMS AND PRINCIPLES

3   Again, me. I'm the author.

DO YOU BELIEVE IN GOD? PROVIDE YOUR REASONING.

4   https://twitter.com/LayahHeilpern/status/1586800646010720256

5   https://twitter.com/shovas/status/1586914566121848832

WE HAVE TO GO BACK

6   http://lostpedia.wikia.com/wiki/Flash_sideways/Theories

7   http://www.amazon.com/Saving-Leonardo-Secular-Assault-Meaning/dp/1433669277

8   http://en.wikipedia.org/wiki/Age_of_Enlightenment

9   http://en.wikipedia.org/wiki/Law_of_noncontradiction

PREPARATION

10   I distinctly recall my thinking more specifically being along the lines of: *If my faith and the bible are true then my faith and the bible will stand up under scrutiny. I will dive into all the atheists' and skeptics' challenges and see if the bible really is right or wrong.*

THOSE WHO MOURN ARE BLESSED: READING SCRIPTURE BACKWARDS.

11   The Author's Note paragraph was part of the original piece and is not new to this book. The referenced piece, 'Be perfect', is included in this book.

BE PERFECT AS YOUR HEAVENLY FATHER IS PERFECT – WAIT, WHAT?

12   https://hermeneutics.stackexchange.com/a/4910/23560

13   *The Book of Matthew is well understood to have been written in Hebrew or Aramaic, to fellow Jews in their own language, but our only surviving manuscripts found so far are in Greek. See:* https://www.catholic.com/qa/was-matthews-gospel-first-written-in-aramaic-or-hebrew

REVELATION

14   Big Death in the Jordan B. Peterson sense of 'catastrophe you can't recover from'.

UNHITCHED: INCEPTION

15   https://www.youtube.com/watch?v=jmoTAtH3zus

16   https://www.youtube.com/watch?v=QBX08olAoFw

17   https://www.youtube.com/watch?v=pShxFTNRCWI

UNHITCHED: AFTERMATH

18   For a particularly excellent reading of Andrea del Sarto, try the following YouTube link or search YouTube for "Andrea del Sarto by Robert Browning (read by Tom O'Bedlam)": https://www.youtube.com/watch?v=Qiw42N_qx_k

About the Author

Matthew James Gallant lives in the Golden Horseshoe of Ontario, Canada where he spends his time enjoying typically Canadian winters, hockey, technology, philosophy, theology, friends, family, and faith.

Matthew grew up in rural 80s Ontario with forests and fields beyond the backyard, and came of age in the 90s around computers, 90s internet-precursor BBSes, and the early internet, itself.

When he can, he enjoys deep, intelligent, stimulating conversation, sports, cars, and road trips.

You can find Matthew at his website and other social media via *mjgallant.ca.*